LOSE WEIGHT

UNLEASH YOUR CREATIVITY

Teachings of Indigenous Healers

How to Transform Your Life

with Nature's Power

Rita Panahi, L.Ac., Dipl.O.M.

ISBN: 978-0-9996648-1-0

First Edition: Mar 2018

10% of all author royalties are donated to the poor

Dedicated to:

My family

&

Nature - that gives us Life

To the Reader

This book is for information purposes only. The author and/or publisher are not accountable or responsible for the use or misuse of the information contained in this book. The book is not intended for medical advice and no claims are made that the information will alleviate health problems. The therapeutic procedures in this book are based on the personal experiences and studies of the author. The author is not responsible for any adverse effects resulting from use of any suggestions made in this book. If you have any medical conditions requiring attention, you should consult with your health care professional regularly, regarding possible modifications of the steps in this book. If you have allergies to certain foods, avoid them.

"Unless the energetic weight that we carry is purified, physical changes to lose weight are often short lived. The secret for that lies in nature."

– Rita Panahi, L.Ac.

Table of Contents

Introduction

My journey to losing weight once and for all and remaining thin was an unexpected and *unusual* one. I want to share with you the unique path that led to my success from a life of constant struggle to lose weight, to a natural and almost effortless weight loss to finally be able to beat the biggest demon of my life. The path that I took over 20 years ago was the missing link for the challenges that I had gone through for over a decade to lose weight. Being thin now, it is often assumed that I have always been this way, when people frequently remark, "You are so lucky that you are naturally thin and have nothing to worry about." What they fail to realize is that like many others, I have been through the constant ups and downs of gaining and losing weight and been through numerous weight loss diets with only temporary results, facing the same frustration, disappointment and hopelessness as everyone else. Losing weight had been difficult; however, maintaining it was just as hard.

The more I saw the numerous diets and the high costs associated with them, which had ended in only temporary results, the more I felt compelled to share my experiences, which have not only been effective, but also lasting. This book will cover weight loss from numerous dimensions, adding aspects that have rarely been addressed, in order to successfully lose weight and keep it off. In addition, I will share the latent power hidden in weight loss to unleash powers within you and untie the knots that have been leading to your downfall in the past, so that the path to losing weight can take you to new levels of yourself, not only physically, but creatively and spiritually as well.

My knowledge comes from numerous sources. I have a Masters in Chinese Medicine, a 5,000-year-old form of natural medicine that views the body holistically, meaning that the body is not separate from the emotions and thoughts, nor from the environment. The foods and drinks that we have not only effect our body, but also our thoughts and emotions. As individuals we are not islands but part of the environment, therefore the seasons of the year, the weather, and the lifestyle that we lead all have a significant impact on us. Having put great emphasis on the healing properties of food and drinks throughout my studies, I realized the power, or in some instances, the curse, that food can be to either heal or destroy one's health and life.

Besides my formal degree, for over 20 years, I worked with indigenous healers, otherwise known as shamans, from numerous cultures. They taught me about their very distinct and strong relationship with nature and their practices that have the healing powers to transform the body, emotions, thoughts, and energy. Living very remotely in the mountains or forests, far away from civilization, they have maintained their rituals and practices with nature for healing and transformation. It was through the teachings that they generously passed on to me that I lost weight so effortlessly and put an end to my lifetime struggle.

This book will be a bridge, bringing the knowledge about how to lose weight, not only as it relates to the physical body, but more importantly, how it relates to the emotions, the thoughts, and our energy together with the energies of nature. I want to invite you to learn a very different and profound perspective for losing weight and keeping it off, through becoming healthy, healing emotionally, finding peace mentally and awakening to your hidden power. Let's start the journey to guide you to discovering the power of weight loss and the magic hidden beneath it, that may be the piece needed for success in losing weight, keeping it off and transforming your self.

"Losing weight does not give us peace. Peace will help us to lose weight. Losing weight will not bring happiness. Happiness will help us make healthy choices so that we lose weight."

- Rita Panahi, L.Ac.

#1

Why Do We Gain Weight?

Bombarded by media advertisements, colorful packaging and sugar added into many products, it takes a lot of strength to not be drawn in like a fish in the water biting the line of cravings and desires. Unfortunately, we are often very susceptible to imprints put in our mind by the environment, television commercials, magazine ads, grocery store bulletins, storefront advertising, our friends and colleagues and our own childhood, especially if we were fed a lot of high-sugar-content food. It is difficult to turn the other way and ignore foods that may be unhealthy, yet taste good, when they are in our face constantly, unless we were to go out into the forest or the mountains where we are not exposed to the temptations.

Marketing is a way to sell products to people and to increase our desires. The seller's concern is to sell a product, not necessarily to keep us healthy. Foods are marketed in such a way to give us an emotion of peace, relaxation, energy, power, and to feel good and happy. The food itself actually does not necessarily do that, but the advertising aims to create the association so that in our mind, we associate the product or food with positive emotions. Much of this happens on such a subtle level that we don't register it consciously. But the results are seen in the number of people who struggle with their weight and in some ways have an addiction to food, using it for comfort, for stress relief and many other purposes other than for hunger.

As a result, losing weight is a multi-million-dollar industry, including fads, diets, supplements, exercise machines, classes, magazines, books, surgery and more. Like puppets with a dangling donut in front of us, we struggle with temptation, our feelings, our willpower and our sense of self worth when we fail and give in to the temptation. We try every new supplement and diet for losing weight, and in some cases even surgery. No matter what we have tried, anyone who has tried to lose weight knows the never-ending battle of taking two steps forward, one step back, five steps forward, three steps back, continuing on and on, with weight loss consuming our mind. It takes a lot of energy to have self control and it's in the moments of weakness, due to stress at work, stress in our relationship, stress with our family, financial stress, emotional stress, stress of transitions in life such as menopause, divorce, separation, death, that we succumb to the temptation and give in, eating the wrong things or overeating.

Our body is a temple, and food, drink and lifestyle choices are the foundation of that temple, which can make it sturdy and strong or make it vulnerable to falling down. As children or even as adults, we were often not taught the impact that food has on our body. We eat anytime that we are hungry and believe eating whatever is labeled as food must be safe and healthy. We were never educated about certain food choices being better and others worse for our overall health and weight. We weren't taught how some foods will improve our quality of life and some can actually worsen it. Never learning about the consequences our choices have, we follow habits and our desires, with our senses being stimulated to the point of becoming almost numb and functioning like a robot, rather than listening to our body. We learn about calories in school but as part of a science class, but never truly understand what it means in real life, unless we are on a fitness or weight loss program. Even when we do learn about it for weight loss, we focus so much on the energy content, in other words, the calories, that we fail to look at the quality of our food. Though weight gain and weight loss are most often associated with food, calories and exercise, there are numerous other factors that are not so readily talked about.

In the same way that we have not understood food choices and its impact on weight, we have also not been taught how to deal with stress and uncomfortable emotions that we experience and their great power over our health. Some of us may not know how to recognize our emotions at all. An emotion can be a feeling of frustration, anger, sadness, anxiety, fear, stress, boredom or worry. It can be just a sensation in the body without a given name as an emotion. Whether the sensation or the emotion can be named or not, when we feel discomfort, there can be a tendency to use food for comfort in order to take the edge off of what we are feeling. We do have a choice as to the reaction we have to our feelings, but oftentimes, when overwhelmed by a feeling, it may feel like we have no choice and before we know it, we find ourselves eating. The bottom line is that we don't use food for what it's intended - nourishing our body - but for ulterior purposes, not recognizing the power of our feelings, nor the power of food. We separate our feelings from our response to those feelings, such as eating even if we are not hungry. We separate food from the impact the food has, such as weight gain. There is a disconnection between our actions and the reactions, cause and effect, root and symptom. The stress that emotions cause leads to a lot of tension in our body, and to ameliorate the discomfort of stress we eat, even if we are not hungry. Tension, stress and excessive negative emotions weaken our digestive system over time. A tense muscle cannot function efficiently and our internal organs are muscles. If we hold our hand as a tight fist for 5 minutes, we will realize it is painful to even open our hand again. This is how negative emotions, tension and stress slow down the efficiency of the digestive system. The more tension they create within our system, the less flow there is, just as the tight fist. In time, this weakens the functions of the body. In order for our body to function optimally, our body needs to be relaxed. A river can only flow if there are no obstructions.

Tensions that we hold onto emotionally, mentally or energetically block the natural flow.

It requires awareness to face our emotions and needs and to catch ourselves before we react instinctively rather than by choice. In the moments when we are unhappy in our life, it may be easier to turn to food rather than deal with our underlying needs. Instead of filling our life with the joy that we are longing for, we can all too easily eat when we feel we cannot attain our goals, thus ultimately pushing our feelings deeper into our unconscious. But the deeper we bury our feelings by overeating, the worse we feel about ourselves and the further we get from our inner self.

The weight that we accumulate becomes an armor of protection, protecting us from our deeper needs as well as from others. For some of us, gaining weight is a way to keep our spouse at a distance because we don't want to be intimate. For others it's a protection to hide our beauty, afraid of the added attention. Or maybe we don't feel worthy of reaching the dreams that we have deep in our heart. Yet for others, it gives a sense of power and authority to have a larger body. There are many underlying reasons for us to protect ourselves through gaining weight. As much as we may consciously want to lose weight, other forces are unconsciously pulling us in the opposite direction.

As we continue reacting and using food as a solution, instead of dealing with the stress or with our emotions and past traumas that lay dormant in our hearts, our energy field becomes more and more polluted. Our body is not merely a physical form but has an energy field expanding beyond what we visually see. Even though we have learned to take a shower daily, we have hardly ever learned how to clear our energy field. The same way that our car collects dust from the environment, our energy field collects the various energies of our environment, from work and family, as well as our past experiences. We can go an entire lifetime never addressing our energy field or even understanding it. The same way that painful emotions and stress can weaken the digestive system over time, is the same way that our energy field, polluted with a lifetime of energies from our own experiences and those of our environment, can weaken not only our digestive system, but also our willpower. Therapy, exercise and eating less can all be helpful, but without addressing the energy field, the results are not complete. The polluted energy field creates such heaviness in our life that no matter what other actions we take to lose weight, it slowly seeps in to weigh us down once again, bringing us back to square one and our old patterns. Among the indigenous people, the energy field is where true lasting transformation begins. They work with nature's energies to clear and heal the energy fields of the years of pollution of past traumas, negative emotions, stress, and habits. The very first step in creating change in order to lose weight is aiming to be healthy, not merely to lose weight. Being healthy involves the body, the emotions, the thoughts as well as the energy.

We will first begin by understanding the value of food and drinks as our primary medicine for transformation, rather than something to quench our desires. Stepping away from dieting, I will guide you to the most critical points to be healthy and reach your goal of losing weight.

"The choices that you make today,
are the consequences that you will need
to deal with tomorrow.
Choose wisely, with the future in mind."
- Rita Panahi, L.Ac.

#2

The Role of Water in Weight Loss

The earth is covered with 70% water. Similarly, our body and blood consists largely of water. The blood carries nutrients into our cells and removes toxins from our cells. When our body doesn't receive sufficient water, the blood flow is gradually compromised, becoming increasingly sluggish with toxins building up in our body. With the cells not receiving enough nutrients and toxins building up, our body functions begin to weaken and become out of balance over time. We feel more fatigue, stiffness in our joints, aches and a whole array of symptoms surface as we support an environment for illness to begin to develop.

Unfortunately we generally give little importance to water, taking it for granted. Some people that I have met have shared with me that they drink merely 1-2 glasses of water per day. They drink coffee or sodas instead and believe that being liquid, they can be a substitute for water. The truth is, nothing is a substitute for pure water. Coffee itself is a diuretic, meaning that it pulls more water out of our body. Juices often have added sugar in them. Most sodas are actually harmful to the body, containing chemicals and large amounts of added sugar, which easily cause weight gain, and those that are low in calories have sugar substitutes but still contain harmful chemicals. Nothing is equal to or can replace pure water for cleansing the body and replenishing the body's liquids.

The deficiency in fluids, water, causes more inflammation in the body and slows down the flow of blood and the body's functions. For example, bowel movements can slow down when we don't drink enough water leading to constipation; in turn constipation leads to a greater buildup of toxicity. The more toxicity that accumulates within the body, the more our mind and our willpower are hindered to make the right choices in our diet and lifestyle. When the bowels are not able to eliminate fully, that in itself also causes more weight gain and a sense of discomfort in the body and how we feel about ourselves. Imagine leaving your dishes with food particles in the sink overnight. The following day, if you try to remove the food stuck to your dishes without using water, it will be very difficult.

But if you soak the dishes for a few minutes, it is extremely easy to clean the dried food remnants from the dishes. It is the same principle inside our body. The body begins the digestive process the moment that we begin to eat. At the end of this process, waste is carried into the intestines to be eliminated. However, when we drink very little water throughout the day, the walls of the intestines gradually become more compromised and waste is not eliminated fully. When this happens, nutrients are also not able to be fully absorbed by the intestinal wall. By drinking sufficient water, we support the lubrication of the intestines for waste to be removed more easily and more fully. Even if we have bowel movements daily, it does not necessarily mean that all of the waste is being fully removed. Contrary to what many believe, that water itself causes more weight gain, in truth, drinking enough water is extremely important in losing weight and supporting the elimination process of the body. The less water we drink, the more the body tries to hold onto the little water that it has. When we drink enough water however, the body is more relaxed and uses the water for the body's functioning and eliminates what is not needed.

As such, water is the first antidote in taking the step toward being healthy. The amount of water that we drink every day is critical in how our entire body functions, including, of course, our metabolism. In order to break down food, not only are enzymes needed, but also the molecules of hydrogen and oxygen, H_2O, which is water. Our cells require water to remove toxins and bring in nutrients. How much water should we drink in a day? Generally about 50% of our body weight in ounces. If you weigh 140 lbs (64 kg), you should drink approximately 70 oz (2 liters) of pure water daily. If you exercise, that amount needs to be even higher because more water is lost through sweating. A good way to remember to drink enough water is to fill a glass bottle with the necessary amount every morning. Then, by the end of the day, you can be sure you have had the correct amount. If the bland taste of water makes it difficult for you to drink such large amounts, then add just a hint of lemon juice or a slice of fruit or cucumber for flavor.

Some people have shared with me that when they drink a lot of water, they find themselves having to urinate a lot more frequently. Of course, putting more water into the body means that more water also needs to leave the body. But if you find yourself having to urinate every hour, that means that the body is not only trying to rid itself of water, but from a Chinese Medicine perspective, it is also ridding itself of excessive heat or inflammation. One of the reasons that heat builds up in our body is due to the lack of water consumption. If we continue not drinking water, then we just add more fire to the fire. We need to drink more, even if it means that we have to urinate more frequently temporarily, in order to bring our body back into balance. The frequency of urination may be high until the excess heat has been neutralized.

The quality of water that we drink must also be considered. Some tap waters are purified under higher standards than others. To be safe, it's best to get a high-quality filter for your home. Refrigerator filters are often not strong enough. In addition, sparkling or carbonated water does not hydrate the body in the same way as still water. Be sure that the amount of water that your body requires is consumed in the form of still, non-carbonated water.

The temperature of the water that you drink is also critical for your body's functions and for losing weight. If you are drinking cold water, you may think that either it doesn't make a difference or that your body uses up energy to warm it up and therefore burns more calories. However, the truth is that based on Chinese Medicine, you are actually weakening your digestive system and the digestion process by drinking cold water and drinks. Digestion doesn't weaken overnight, but gradually. Inside of the body, the stomach needs to maintain a certain temperature to function. When you put cold water or drinks into your body, it may feel good in the moment, but until the stomach has returned back to its ideal temperature it will not be able to digest properly and efficiently and the food begins fermenting. This is one of the reasons for bloating, gas and constipation. Therefore, it is best to drink only room temperature or hot water, and this applies to other drinks as well, such as juices, smoothies, teas, etc. It is better for your overall health and a further support for losing weight.

Although drinking enough water throughout the day is important, drinking it at certain times can be more beneficial for losing weight. Start your morning with a cup of hot water. Doing this will start your body cleansing first thing in the morning. Throughout the day, always drink a glass of water about 15 minutes *before* eating your meals. This will reduce the need for over-eating by filling your stomach and cleansing the pathway before the food follows. If you are thirsty while eating your meal, have only small sips, in order to not dilute the digestive enzymes, so that the food can be better digested. At times we mistake the signals that our body is giving us, misinterpreting the signal for thirst with hunger. Instead of drinking something to quench our thirst, we eat, even though we may have just eaten. When we are hungry, it is good to ask ourselves if it's truly hunger or if we are dehydrated and need to drink more water. In either situation, it is better to first have a glass of water. After that we will know if we are still hungry or if water was what our body really needed.

We are often more concerned about losing weight in relation to our appearance; however, what we need to realize is that our body is not healthy when we are carrying too much extra weight. This is even more important for us to focus on in the long run. Our organ functions become weaker from having to digest large quantities of food as well as the wrong type of foods leading to many health conditions. In addition, excessive weight can put extra pressure on our knees and lower back causing pain. The consequences that excessive weight has on our health are tremendous. This is the reason why it's more important to focus on becoming healthy rather than simply losing weight. The thought of losing weight can become an immense pressure for success and failure, whereas focusing on being healthy can be empowering in the long run.

"The amount of water that we drink every day is critical in how our entire body functions, including of course, our metabolism."

- Rita Panahi, L.Ac.

#3

Foods from the Earth

L iving food receives energy from the sun, the soil, the water and air in order to grow. Through this process it becomes rich in nutrients and nourishes us when we eat it. When we look at the vast shapes and colors of produce, we can only feel awe at the beauty of living foods. It's a world of wonder; the orange and green colors of a carrot and its stem, the purple color of eggplants, the red and green color of apples and the amazing shapes and colors of corn, wheat, quinoa, lemons, raspberries, broccoli, asparagus and on and on. We need to appreciate where our food has come from, the time it has taken for it to grow and the power source that it is. Even though we buy a cabbage from a grocery store or a market, it was harvested from the earth and took many days to grow before it was ready for us to consume it. If we lose touch with that, we may not truly value our food. Drinking coconut juice fresh from inside of a coconut is very different from drinking a soda from a can filled with sugar, chemicals and additives.

In our fast-paced, quick-fix world, it is easy to lose touch with where our food comes from and real whole foods. Some of us may have never heard of certain vegetables or legumes, nor do we know what they even look or taste like. We may know the newest designer dress or the newest computer in the market, but not know what okra, mung beans, or chard are. Our foods come in so many colorful packages, and the ingredients have been so transformed that they no longer look like the original form of the food anymore.

Many salad dressings have soy in them, but we may never have seen a soy bean in real life. Many chips are made from corn, but we may never have eaten corn on the cob in its natural form. Food is meant for nourishment, for us to have energy, to help our structure to be strong, and to keep us alive and healthy. Whole foods provide this for our body.

Influenced largely by a fast-paced world and fast food, many of us may not be familiar with all of the choices that we have when it comes to grains, legumes, vegetables, fruits, nuts and seeds. I want to share a list (though incomplete) of some whole foods, so that you can appreciate the beauty and choices available.

Fruits	Fruits	Vegetables	Vegetables
Apple	Mangosteen	Asparagus	Turnip
Banana	Papaya	Chard	Bitter Melon
Pineapple	Durian	Kale	Kohlrabi
Mango	Kumquat	Spinach	Parsnip
Orange	Mandarin	Arugula	Rutabaga
Tangelo	Quince	Collard green	Leek
Grapefruit	Lychee	Broccoli	Endive
Lime	Longan	Cauliflower	Squash
Lemon	Mulberry	Okra	Kabocha
Kiwi	Guava	Jicama	Pumpkin
Pear	Date	Bok-Choy	Yam
Peach	Pomegranate	Brussel	Sweet Potato
Nectarine	Persimmon	sprouts	Potato
Plum	Fig	Beets	Daikon radish
Apricot	Watermelon	Cabbage	Radish
Blueberries	Canteloupe	Artichoke	Carrot
Raspberries	Grapes	Eggplant	Bell Pepper
Strawberry		Celery	Zucchini
Cherry		Fennel	

Grains	Legumes	Nuts	Seeds
White Rice	Black-eyed	Walnut	Pumpkin
Brown Rice	peas	Almond	Sesame
Wild Rice	Mung bean	Brazil nuts	Sunflower
Quinoa	Aduki bean	Pecan	Chia
Spelt	Black bean	Cashew	Flax
Oats	Garbanzo bean	Macadamia	Poppy
Barley	Lentil	Pine nuts	
Buckwheat	Kidney bean	Pistachio	
Corn	Soy bean	Hazelnut	
Millet	Lima bean	Chestnut	
Wheat	Navy bean		
Rye	Chickpeas		
Amaranth	Pinto bean		
	Split peas		

Whole foods grow using the life force of nature. They are even more beneficial when they are organically grown. Our body is made to assimilate natural foods. We can break down whole foods more efficiently than processed foods and receive more nutrients from them. Processed foods are not only oftentimes stripped of their nutrients, but have many added chemicals, preservatives and sometimes colors that are harmful to the body. Whenever chemicals and additives are introduced into the body, whether this is as a result of processed foods or non-organic foods that have been treated with harmful pesticides or genetically modified (GMO), we are giving added strain to our digestive system. This added strain weakens and slows down our metabolism and digestive capacity, leading to an increased toxicity in our body. Processed foods also do not have the same life force and nutritional richness as whole foods do, partially due to the fact that they have been stripped of this in the manufacturing process, but also because of the body's inability to efficiently process the food and receive all of the nutrients that it might have. Some processed foods are simply for taste and have really no value to the body, and in some cases are causing more harm than good in the long run.

What are we talking about when speaking about processed foods? For example, potato chips, candy, soda, muffins, donuts, cookies, cakes, fast food, milk shakes. These are only some examples of processed foods. Yet even certain breads and pastas have been stripped of a lot of the nutrition in addition to having preservatives and chemicals added in their ingredients.

The real purpose of food is to nourish our body and keep us healthy and strong throughout our lifetime; however, food has become a product used for advertising, regardless of whether it is truly beneficial for us or not. If all of the money that was spent on commercials and packaging would be spent on growing more whole organic foods and encouraging healthy food choices, we would all be in a much better place with our overall health and less dependent on medications.

Whole foods sometimes come in packaging as well. They are not always fresh. You can buy produce frozen, canned or dried. When you have a choice, it is best to buy fresh foods without any packaging. The next best choice would be either dried or frozen and lastly canned. Canned food comes in a can that sometimes has lead, aluminum or other metals, which can leach into the food itself. This is not the case for all cans, but many. If you must choose canned foods, foods in glass jars are better. In general though, canned foods, whether in a jar or a can may have preservatives added as well.

For losing weight, whole foods are better than processed foods. You will be able to get more nutrients from them and be able to more efficiently digest whole foods, putting less of a burden on your body from the chemicals and additives put into processed foods. The majority of the time you will also be consuming much less calories when eating whole foods rather than processed foods. Therefore, an important part of losing weight is to eat whole foods and decrease or avoid processed foods as much as possible. If you avoid processed and junk food for a few days, you will notice the difference in how you feel. When you eat chocolate or processed food, you may initially feel good because of the taste, however, that feeling is only temporary. The negative effects can show up hours or sometimes days later with such symptoms as headaches, weight gain, constipation, foggy mind, fatigue and more. Processed foods in general can also lead to more inflammation in the body. When you eat whole foods, you create more long-lasting, positive benefits for your health.

Many processed foods have sugar added in their ingredients. Any food that contains sugar or is converted to sugar can often be used as a comfort food, to help us relax or to give us the nurturing that we are lacking in the moment. There is a difference in the types of sugar that we consume. Sugar from fruits, consumed in moderation, is considered healthy. Brown rice, which is a form of carbohydrate and converted to sugar, is healthy. Our body requires carbohydrates to fulfill the body's immediate energy requirements. However, sugar in soda, muffins, chocolate and processed foods, is not healthy. Unfortunately, once we turn to these latter types of sugar, our body begins to crave it even more, leading to an addictive desire, which makes the road of return almost impossible. Vegetables are the best food to break the vicious cycle of sugar addiction. With vegetables being more alkaline, they can neutralize the acidity caused by too much sugar intake, as well as reduce the sugar craving as they cleanse our body. Vegetables are the best source for countering sweet cravings. They are filled with nutrients and apart from nourishing your body, they are like a broom that cleanse your intestines. No matter how frequent or infrequent your bowel movements are, vegetables help to remove the debris that may be stuck to the intestinal wall without us even being aware of it. It's unfortunate that vegetables have such a bad reputation and are therefore disliked, because they are one of the most important foods for weight loss.

Inadvertently, many think of salads when the word vegetable is used. While green leafy salads are also a vegetable, they consist mainly of water and roughage. They are great to eat, though in moderation. What I am referring to here are the many other wonderful vegetables such as carrots, asparagus, brussel sprouts, broccoli, daikon radish, sweet potato and celery, to name a few. For weight loss and general health, it is important to eat a *large* bowl of mixed steamed vegetables with at least one meal or even as a meal once daily. Just as water intake is underestimated, so too is vegetable intake. Too many people have shared with me that they are either not eating any vegetables (thinking salads are enough) or they are eating only a small amount on the side and frequently the same one or two vegetables. In order to lose weight, vegetables must become a part of our daily diet, and not just in small amounts, but large amounts (approximately 6-8 cups daily). Choose 2-3 different vegetables daily, alternate the choices daily and steam them.

Though eating raw vegetables does give us more nutrients that may be lost when overcooking foods, when we have gained weight, it is already a sign that our digestive system has become weaker, therefore eating too many raw foods on a regular basis can be much more taxing on our system. Some vegetables are very difficult to digest if they are eaten raw such as, kale, cabbage and broccoli. It is best, at the very least, to lightly steam vegetables before eating them.

When it comes to fruits, many of us are used to eating them as snacks or as a light dessert after a meal. Though fruits are healthy, whole foods, the timing of eating them is important in weight loss. Fruits, if eaten following a meal or with other foods as snacks, cause fermentation to take place. Fresh fruits generally require only 30-45 minutes to be broken down through the digestive process, whereas most other foods, including dried fruits, require 2-6 hours. The sugar from fruit, especially those that are higher in their sugar content, causes fermentation when eaten with another food that has a much higher time requirement for being broken down. This can lead to bloating, gas and oftentimes constipation. Not only will this cause a feeling of discomfort, but it will also cause waste to remain in the body for a longer period of time. Over time, this weakens the digestive system leading to weight gain.

When we have been in the habit of eating processed foods or overeating, sometimes we feel we want to just stop time and start over and wish we could simply press the reset button. The best way to do this is by doing gentle cleanses throughout the year. One of the key foods to cleanse and reset the body with are vegetables, both in their whole form or as a juice.

Juicing is a great way to obtain nutrients, feel energized and cleanse the body of excess toxins and waste. A great practice to have as part of our weekly routine can be to start the day 2-3 times per week by drinking an organic vegetable juice. You can mix in carrots, beets, kale, chard, celery and parsley, as an example. Be creative and create your own favorite juice combination. Just remember that because you are taking in a high concentration of vegetables at one time in a liquid form, you need to dilute it with water and drink it slowly, as if you were chewing it. Juice your own vegetables whenever possible; however, when you feel pressed for time, feel free to buy organic refrigerated juices as a substitute. Avoid canned juices. They generally have added preservatives, which will defeat the purpose of you trying to clear your body of toxins.

Cleansing should be a part of our weight loss plan as well as your long-term health goal. When it comes to cleansing, I believe that a gradual gentle cleanse is always more effective than an extreme harsh one. Fasting for many days on water may cause you to lose weight temporarily, but it will all come back as soon as you start eating again because your body, having been starved, begins to panic and overeat the moment it is allowed to again. It's true that our body needs a rest, but it's better to do it gently in order to have long-term lasting results.

The cleanse that I will share with you is one that I have found to be the most gentle yet beneficial to help reset your body and clear accumulated waste. Once or twice a year, take 7-10 days to do a cleanse. You can also do parts of this cleanse on a weekend to give your body a rest once a month.

Here are the guidelines for the cleanse below:

DON'TS

No meat – which includes chicken, turkey, pork, duck, beef – basically all animal meats.

No fish.

No dairy – which includes milk, cheese, yogurt, ice cream, butter.

No chips, chocolates, donuts, breads, pasta, muffins, donuts, crackers, candy.

No alcohol, soda, energy drinks, coffee or black tea.

No nuts or nut butters.

No pasta.

No sugar, jam, dried fruits.

No iced drinks.

No hot spices such as pepper, chili, jalapeño.

No salad dressings (lemon juice and olive oil are ok).

DO'S

Drink a minimum of 2-3 liters (64-90 oz.) or more (based on your body weight) of room temperature, still water every day.

Drink a glass of hot or warm water first thing in the morning.

All that you eat and drink must be organic.

Take a high-quality probiotic twice a day, once before bedtime and once upon awakening.

Steps for the cleanse, based on a 10-day plan:

Day 1 + 2 eat ONLY long-grain rice, small beans, vegetables and fruits (mung beans are a good choice for beans).

Day 3 + 4 eat ONLY vegetables and fruits (no bananas, no dried fruits, no raisins).

Day 5 + 6 drink only liquids such as vegetable juice (dilute and drink it slowly), broth from vegetables, fresh juiced fruits (dilute and drink it slowly) and herbal teas.

Day 7 + 8 eat ONLY vegetables and fruits (no dried fruits, no raisins).

Day 9 + 10 eat ONLY brown rice, small beans, veggies and fruits (mung beans are a good choice for beans).

After completing the cleanse, be careful about what you eat. Don't go directly into poor habits.

Instead, introduce harder-to-digest foods such as nuts, meat, fish and cheese very gradually and in small amounts. The purpose of the cleanse is to help reset your body and give you extra encouragement to continue eating healthy with improved choices. Sometimes the reset button needs to be hit more frequently to get us into more healthy habits. Following the suggestions below will help you to reset your body throughout the year, rather than just once. Each time that you do, you will gain more strength to eat healthier throughout the year and feel better until it becomes a habit. At the beginning, you may feel a withdrawal from the processed foods and unhealthy habits that you were accustomed to. In time you may find a withdrawal when you are *not* eating healthy! When I was young, I used to love ice cream and crave it quite frequently. It is amazing that now, I crave vegetables when I am traveling and don't have access to a kitchen to cook a lot of vegetables on a daily basis. Our actions are all based on habits. Indeed, it is possible to change them to healthier ones.

On a daily basis, you should start your morning off with a cup of hot, pure water. You should also eat a large bowl of mixed steamed vegetables for lunch or dinner.

On a weekly basis, you should incorporate a few vegetables and juice them, adding extra water to dilute it and drinking it slowly.

On a monthly basis, you should take 1-2 days, maybe on a weekend or your day off, and eat pure whole foods, consisting mainly of vegetables, fruits, light soups and juicing.

On a yearly basis, you should take 7-10 days, once or twice a year and do a full gentle cleanse following the steps given above.

All of these will help to reset your system to a fresh start and give you the necessary strength to follow a healthier life as you lose weight. Remember, it's not just about losing weight, it's about being healthy, and losing weight comes naturally when you are eating healthy. Each time that you do a cleanse, whether it's a short one on a weekend or a longer one, you are allowing your body to become revitalized and renewed. That feeling will encourage you to continue making healthier choices.

"The very first step in creating change in order to lose weight is aiming to be healthy, not merely to lose weight."

- Rita Panahi, L.Ac.

#4

Beyond Energy In.
Energy Out.

When it comes to weight loss, calories and exercise are the topics that are most frequently talked about. What are calories? Calories are a way to describe energy. Our body requires energy to function and the calorie amount in a food is the energy content of the food. It's simple math. To give an example, your body, based on your activity on a normal day, your constitution, weight and height, may require 2500 calories per day. If you eat 4000 calories of food, you will have given your body an extra 1500 calories that it will now need to store, and it generally stores it as fat. On the other hand, if you require 2500 calories per day and only eat 2000 calories of food, your body will now be short by 500 calories, which it requires for its daily activity. It will need to get the extra 500 calories from your stored energy by burning the stored fat. As such, if your goal is to lose weight, the general idea is that you need to eat less calories than what you require or burn more calories than what you have eaten, which can be done by participating in more activity.

Looking back at our first example, if you require 2500 calories for your daily functioning but you have eaten 4000 calories, if you do not want the remaining 1500 to be stored as fat, then you need to do more activity, equaling to the 1500 calories to be able to, at the very least, maintain your weight.

Many of us are not aware of the actual amount of calories in the food that we are consuming. We underestimate the number of calories based on the size of the food or the amount we have eaten. For example, nuts are very small, but they are harder to digest and high in calories compared to vegetables which can be quite large in size, but easier to digest and lower in calories.

Let me share some examples so that you can compare the difference of calories for the same amount of different foods (these are approximate numbers only):

Food (250g):	Calories:
Almonds	1440 calories
Sunflower butter	1542 calories
Broccoli	85 calories
Cabbage	62 calories
Black-eyed peas	225 calories
Lentils	290 calories
Chicken	598 calories
Peach	98 calories
Raisins	748 calories
Grapes	168 calories
White rice	325 calories
Quinoa	357 calories

You can see the enormous difference in calories for the same 250 grams of each food. There are apps that you can download that will tell you the number of calories in each food. I would advise making a list of the foods that you eat most often as a chart with the number of calories they contain. This allows you to see more objectively how many calories you are actually consuming daily. However, calories consumed and calories used are only one part of weight loss. Numerous other factors also need to be addressed.

It is important to note that, just because a whole food is harder to digest or higher in calories, it does not mean that it is not healthy. Nuts, for example, are a healthy form of fat, but they should be eaten in moderation. Nuts specifically, are also better digested if they have been soaked for a few hours in pure water, before being consumed.

Beyond calories, maintaining a balance between rest and activity is also crucial. We assume that we need to be active all of the time in order to use up as many calories as possible. But just as the body needs some level of healthy activity, it also requires enough rest. Sleep is a critical part of weight loss. If the body does not have the time to replenish itself, which is the purpose of sleep, then it cannot function optimally and over time it becomes weaker. Sleep is essential for the body to rejuvenate and recover. We need to learn to listen to our body in order to know when it's signaling us to stop and rest and when it needs to be active. Just as lack of activity is harmful to the body, so too is a lack of sufficient rest. The body absolutely needs to sleep enough hours. There may be times under special circumstances that we only sleep 4 hours, but if that continues on a daily basis, the tension that it causes our body will weaken our digestive system and slow down the removal of toxins and waste. There are no fixed rules for how many hours you should sleep, but from my experience in seeing health issues with my patients, I have found that a minimum of 6-8 hours is needed every night. Remember, life is about balance. By honoring our body and balancing rest and activity, we support our health and keep our body's metabolism strong.

Due to excess stress in their lives, some people drink alcohol in order to relax their body and mind. But alcohol, though it initially may have a relaxing effect, is high in sugar. It is a form of empty calories, meaning a lot of calories from a very small amount of liquid. In the long run, it also weakens our ability to sleep deeply. Alcohol gets processed by the liver and in Chinese Medicine, the liver is in charge of the free flow of qi or energy in the body. Over time, continuous intake of alcohol will make the liver more sluggish, which means the ability to remove toxins from our body will be slowed down. With increased toxins, the digestive system becomes weaker. The consequences of frequent consumption of alcohol can be seen starting from the simple increase in calories, leading to the buildup of toxicity due to the liver becoming more impacted, weakening of the digestive process from the buildup of toxicity, and sleep being compromised in the long run, ultimately all leading to gradual weight gain.

Eating very late in the evening also impacts our quality of sleep. When we eat late, the body has to work in order to digest the food that we have eaten, instead of resting. Foods require varying amounts of time to digest. Fruits and vegetables require much less time to digest than meats and nuts. Depending on our food choices, food combination and the size of our meal, our body will not be able to sleep deeply if we eat late in the evening because of needing to process the food instead. The quality of our sleep is important, and what we eat and drink before sleeping as well as the time that we eat all impact the quality. Therefore, in order to lose weight, it is best to eat before 7pm, if we go to sleep at 11pm or later. This allows the body enough time to break down the food while we are still awake rather than when we are sleeping. Our body is then able to fast and rest for 10-12 hours so that the food from our previous day can be more fully digested. If your lifestyle does not allow for you to eat by 7pm, then let your last meal of the day before sleep be your lightest meal, avoiding meat, fish, fried foods, dairy, nuts, fast food, processed food and alcohol, and keeping your portion small.

The state of our mind before going to bed also affects the quality of our sleep. If we bring our day's stress and worry to bed, in the same way that our body has to digest our dinner when it's eaten late, it will have to process all of the information in our mind. Similarly, watching television right up to the point before going to bed or falling asleep while watching television affects our mind, and ultimately the quality of our sleep and our metabolism. The constant stimulation from the television does not allow our mind to be in a relaxed state. If you are unable to sleep and use the television to relax your mind, similar to those that use alcohol for the same purpose, it is important to reflect on the underlying cause that has led to your inability to relax, rather than using either alcohol or television as a band-aid solution for relaxation. Taking 5-10 minutes to meditate before going to bed and letting our thoughts become silent will support us more and have more deep-rooted results. Therefore, to improve the quality of your sleep, quiet your mind, relax your body, turn off the television and go to bed in a peaceful state.

Stress has a direct impact on our metabolism. A stressed body is a tense body, and where there is tension there is less flow. When there is less flow, digestion becomes compromised and greater toxicity accumulates, creating more stagnation, and ultimately less nourishment can be received by the cells. Sleep, meditation, and breathing deeply are vital to relieving stress. When we are stressed, our sleep is compromised, our body becomes more tense, and our breathing becomes more shallow. Yet in order for our body to function optimally, it requires that we breathe deeply to bring in oxygen more fully. Sometimes exercising too hard can also lead us to shallow breathing. Spend at least 10 minutes breathing deeply into your abdomen, or go for a walk for 20 minutes in the fresh air and breathe deeply, taking in the life force of the earth. This will greatly improve your metabolism and help you to lose weight.

Life is about energy, and weight loss and weight gain are about energy in and energy out. However, though food is energy, the quality of the food makes a significant difference if we want to be healthy along with losing weight. Not every food has the same number of calories. Not every food, even if it has the same amount of calories, is easy on the digestive system, depending on how much time it requires for digestion, whether it's organic or has harmful chemical pesticides, whether its GMO, whether its processed or a whole food. Organic foods will be easier on the body than non-organic or GMO foods. Whole foods will be easier on the body than processed foods. And in addition, the quality of our sleep, our environment, our lifestyle choices, our emotional state and energy also play a role in how well we digest our food and how strong our metabolism is.

Our body isn't only assimilating the food that we eat, but also the environment and people that we interact with. Just as certain foods are easier and harder to digest or certain foods are healthier or not as healthy for us, there are experiences of life that are also easier and harder to digest, healthier or not as healthy for us, and those will impact our physical digestion and weight gain or loss as well. We will go deeper into this in the chapters ahead.

"It's unfortunate that vegetables have such a bad reputation and are therefore disliked, because they are one of the most important foods for weight loss. Vegetables are the best food to break the vicious cycle of sugar addiction."

- Rita Panahi, L.Ac.

#5

Food as Protection

When we are confronted with difficult circumstances in life, our natural instinct may be to protect ourselves. Such circumstances can arise when we are exposed to pollution in our environment and food or when we are exposed to people or situations that cause us pain. If we feel physically threatened by someone, our natural reaction is to hide or put our arms up to protect ourselves. Our body responds in the same manner when it is exposed to environmental pollutants that it does not know how to deal with or certain people or situations that cause us pain.

Instinctively, our body tries to protect us from anything that it perceives as harmful or a threat. For some of us, this protection comes in the form of gaining weight. Weight serves as a barrier or a fortress of protection, both physically and emotionally.

When we eat foods with chemical pesticides that are not natural to our digestive system, the body, unable to fully eliminate the toxins, keeps them latent hidden within fat cells to prevent them from causing harm to the body. It is like building an enclosure around a perceived enemy. The enemy is not destroyed but it is kept under control, at least for the time being. If the toxins increase over time, the fortress, unable to keep them under control infinitely, breaks down and more severe health issues ensue. The toxins need to be released from the body or they will begin to cause greater damage gradually. Many of the foods that we eat, if not organic, have chemical pesticides sprayed on them. In addition, we are bombarded with food colorings and preservatives in most foods. Body products that we use on our skin and hair similarly contain many harmful chemicals that are absorbed by the skin. If we were exposed to these only once in a while, our body would be able to eliminate it more readily. However, if we are exposed to one thing or another in our food or body products on a daily basis, the body becomes overwhelmed and it becomes very difficult for the body to eliminate it all.

Heavy metals are another form of toxin that we need to deal with regularly, whether it's from the mercury fillings in our teeth, the types of pots we use to cook with, the canned food that we purchase or the fish that we eat. We can have BPA leaching into our drinks from plastic bottles left in the heat in our cars, mimicking our hormones and changing the hormonal balance of our body. In one way or another, it seems that our food and body products do not have the purity that they should have and they are what we put in or on our body on a daily basis.

Toxins build gradually over time and from Chinese Medicine perspective, fat cells try to protect us by keeping their adverse impact latent so that they don't cause more severe harm to our system and health. But the protection is only temporary, not a long-term solution for our health. As we talked about earlier, we need to do a cleanse regularly in order to rid our body of toxins. As we cleanse our body however, the toxins that have remained latent may show new symptoms in our body during the process of eliminating them. As the protective barrier begins to reduce, we may experience what is called a healing crisis. A healing crisis occurs when the body goes through a significant change as it purges the latency of many years. During this purging, we may for example temporarily experience headaches, diarrhea, body-ache on a physical level or have very old emotions surfacing. Whatever the body had formed a protective layer around slowly begins to release while losing weight. If we are not prepared to face the emotions or the detoxification of our body, we might become fearful and that may hinder our progress.

In Chinese medicine it is said that we not only digest food, but also the experiences of our life. Emotions, just like food, need to be digested and both can either empower us to be strong and fit or weaken us and make us sick and gain weight.

Situations that are difficult for us to digest emotionally are also hard on our digestive system. If we are faced with too much trauma or emotional pain, it is like overeating or eating too much junk food; it eventually weakens our digestive system as well. Experiencing certain emotions, such as anger, fear, grief, or worry on a regular basis can be highly toxic for our body. They will weaken the energetics of our organs and slow down and weaken their function. As the organs energetics become weaker, their ability to process food also becomes weaker, leading to a greater tendency for weight gain. Excessive worry weakens our ability to digest, excessive anger creates more stress and tension in the body, excessive grief weakens us. All emotions impact the body, and when in excess, will have side effects the same way as eating too much chocolate or drinking too much alcohol will have side effects. Many times people wonder why they are not losing weight when they are hardly eating anything. One of the reasons is that they are not taking into consideration their emotional state and their home or work environment and how it is impacting their health, their metabolism and their peace of mind. In the same way that negative emotions impact our health and weight negatively, internal happiness and peace strengthen our body and digestive ability.

Every day, we wake up, drive to work through the traffic, have meetings, go to a restaurant surrounded by people, come home and turn on the television exposing ourselves to news and advertisments, talk to friends who share their pains with us and eventually go to bed. In every single interaction, we have been exposed to many energies and emotions that we need to digest. Our food, drinks, the people we interacted with, the activities we undertook, the air, and the environment have all been "food" for our body and mind. All of them have impacted our state of mind, our emotions and ultimately our metabolism in one way or another.

When we feel overwhelmed by our environment, our own feelings, or the toxins in our food, our body protects us by gaining weight as a defense mechanism. Of course, not everybody responds this way to the stressors of life. But for those who gain weight easily, most likely, that is their defense mechanism. Anything that has been too difficult to face or 'digest' emotionally becomes latent in our body energetically through the protective layer that we create around us by gaining weight. One of the main reasons that we gain weight quickly after dieting and losing weight is because we have not faced our emotions and their weight in our life. The body, in the same manner as before, gains weight as a protective shield, in order to repress the painful emotions and make them latent once again. Negative emotions and traumas are heavy energetically and weigh us down just as physical weight does. They are interconnected and impact each other greatly and when the heavy emotional weight is not addressed or healed, it can be the undercurrent that does not allow us to lose weight and keep it off.

As children, we may have been raised learning to hold our emotions in without expressing them to anyone and sometimes not even acknowledging them to ourselves. We were taught to keep quiet and not speak up if we are unhappy, or to remain quiet when we are angry. Though practicing self control and not hurting others by expressing our negative emotions can have its advantages, if we hold our emotions inside and don't face them even within our own consciousness, we may turn the anger or unhappiness towards our own self and hurt our own self by overeating or drinking alcohol as a way of repressing the feelings even more. We need to first be aware of our emotions and how they are affecting us so that we don't turn to food in order to repress them. We also need to learn to deal with the root of the emotions so that they don't remain dormant like volcanoes ready to erupt at any given time and hurt either others or ourselves. Remember that emotions also impact our digestive system. The heavier the emotion is, the stronger the impact on our digestive system. Emotions leave stains within our body that need to be cleared fully at the root so that they don't have power over our life and our health.

To lose weight and keep it off, it's important to be honest with ourselves, with our emotions and our pain, and see how our weight is serving us so that we can develop healthier patterns. Sometimes we gain weight as a protective layer to keep people at a distance. I have met people who have told me that they don't love themselves or don't feel beautiful and use gaining weight as a way to keep people at a distance, proving even more that they are unlovable. Others have shared their resistance to being physically intimate with their spouse and they found gaining weight as a means of making themselves less desirable. Sometimes, having been shamed about our sexuality or the powerful energy that sexual energy has, we gain weight to repress those emotions, especially if we are without a partner or if sexuality is in some way a taboo for us. If we have experienced abuse in the past, we may use the excess weight to prevent others from approaching us. We may have needs in our life that have gone unfulfilled such as the need to feel loved, the need for affection or admiration, or the need to feel closeness. When these needs remain unfulfilled, we may create a barrier around ourselves by gaining weight as a way to numb those feelings. Of course, all of these patterns are often times quite unconscious until we delve deeper into our emotions. Emotions are merely energy and they can be transformed. First however, we need to be aware of their existence and their impact on our lives.

Ultimately, gaining weight is serving a purpose that we may not be fully aware of consciously and we use it as a form of boundary of protection around us. Many situations in life may be too difficult to face, and by gaining weight we keep ourselves stuck, not able to grow and transform. It's important to ask ourselves what we are protecting ourselves from either externally or internally so that we can begin to move the energy internally through our awareness. Are we protecting ourselves from someone we are afraid of? Are we protecting ourselves from our own pain? How would we feel different if we lost weight and what kind of attention or changes would it bring about in our relationship with the world? Would we be expected to be more active with the family and no longer complain of having knee pain? Would we be more sexually appealing and be sought after more often by our spouse or the opposite sex? Would we need to let go of the pattern of self hate or self sacrifice? Would we be free to express our power and energy through work or other activity? Even though some of these scenarios can seem quite appealing, for some of us, they can also be frightening.

Gaining and losing weight brings about many changes, not only for our physical body, but for our emotions and our relationship with ourselves and the world. We may not make the connection about how it serves or doesn't serve us to be heavier or thinner, but we need to reflect on the benefits and disadvantages of both. Weight loss creates changes and if we are afraid of those changes, we can prevent ourselves from reaching our goal. When we rid ourselves of toxins through our diet and cleansing and when we face and heal our emotions, weight loss can be more lasting.

"Gaining weight often serves as a fortress of protection from our emotions and our environment"

- Rita Panahi, L.Ac.

#6

Anxiety and Change

Change can be very frightening to many of us. It means possibly having to face the unknown and all of the uncertainty that it can bring along with it. Uncertainty can trigger anxiety in many of us. We prefer grounding and stability, and when change comes, it can feel like the rug has been pulled from under us. In truth, anxiety is like an internal fire within that we are afraid of. It is a fire with tremendous power that is encouraging us to change. In fact, anxiety and excitement are very similar energies, though at first, they may not feel that way. Excitement is something one feels about a change that one believes will be positive and looks forward to. Anxiety is often a signal for a change that is needed but resisted because one is uncertain of the outcome. That change may be an external change, such as changing one's home or job, a family member's health, or it could be an internal change such as changing one's outlook or learning to deal with a situation that one doesn't have clear answers for. Sometimes we consciously make choices for change. Sometimes life nudges us to change even if we are resistant to it. Change requires energy. Both excitement and anxiety are like a fire giving us energy for change. If we are anxious about the change, we feel discomfort in handling this energy and may use food to repress it, like putting water on fire to reduce its flames. What happens though, when we use food to repress this internal fire, is that it never actually puts it out. Instead it makes the fire latent in our body, like an inferno that can erupt and destroy our health gradually. Energy needs to flow. Anytime the energy is repressed by eating, we are blocking this natural flow of growth and transformation by gaining weight. The weight serves as a way to ground the energy and ground us, in order to control and prevent this powerful force that has the potential for creativity to bring change in our life.

There are many stages in life that we naturally go through that bring about change, starting from being a child to when we become a teenager and onto the various phases of adulthood and ending at old age. Each stage is about growth, not only physically but also emotionally, creatively and spiritually. Instead of honoring the power of our transformation, out of anxiety, we may fight it, using food to take the edge off of the challenges. For example, as a teenager, we face the changes our body goes through during puberty, such as our view of our self, our body, the new attention we may receive from the opposite sex, the sexual energy that we are not familiar with experiencing. As adults we might feel the need to excel to another level in our job or try something completely different that actually makes us happy. As we get even older we might have to deal with divorce and death. The sadness of loss can be so severe that we turn to food to fill the emptiness in our life. These phases can be exciting or anxiety producing. Excitement means feeling fully alive and living our inner gifts, however it can be just as frightening for some of us to feel fully alive as it is for others to face life changes or the traumas of the past. Just as any drug is used to escape, both pain and vitality, food is often used to escape the ups and downs of life.

Our habits often begin when we are very young, when we cried and our caretakers didn't understand what we needed. To calm us down and stop us from crying, they may have given us food, usually in the form of sweets. If our parents didn't have the time to cook, we may have been given something easy and comforting such as a peanut butter and jelly sandwich. As a result, we learned early on that sweets can take the place of our emotional needs, calm our upset emotions, and quench the fire of our exuberant energy. Food has frequently been used as a band-aid to temper either our own or our children's energy or discomfort.

Life can throw an unexpected curveball at us, a sudden loss of a job or a loss of a relationship. Unhappy with the situation and resisting the change, we may turn the anger toward ourselves and overeat or eat all of the things that are not truly nourishing for our body, as opposed to facing our frustration and accepting a new beginning in our life. We feel anxious about what's ahead. The unexpected change in our life has released the energy for a new opportunity for growth, and instead of embracing the change, our anxiety can have us turn to food to slow down that process.

In all of these situations, food is used as a drug and in the same manner, we become addicted to it. It's never healthy to be overweight. It's never healthy to eat too much sugar, chips, junk food, etc. Yet we often grab the easiest drug there is, food, to escape. All addictions are compensations for deeper emotional wounds, unfulfilled needs, and anxiety about the unknown that we are trying to escape. All drugs ultimately harm us. In the same way, overeating or eating too much of the wrong foods will harm us as well, not only physically, but also emotionally and on our path to personal growth. It may fulfill its purpose in the moment, but in the long run, if it becomes a habit, it will have great consequences. It's much easier to gain weight than it is to lose it. Rather than eating when we are actually hungry and stopping when we have reached satiation, we eat excessively, out of habit, without listening to the internal wisdom of our body communicating with us.

We regularly misunderstand many of the signals that the body gives us. If we are thirsty, we eat instead of drinking water. If we are tired, we eat to get energy. If we are nervous, we eat to calm our anxiety. If we are stressed, we eat to calm and relax ourselves. One signal has nothing to do with the action we are taking, but out of habit, we mistakenly eat instead of responding with what is actually needed. All of these responses come from habits and habits can be relearned. When we respond habitually, we become like a feather blown off of the ground with the slightest wind, losing our ground by the circumstances of life.

Generally, those of us who are more sensitive to our surroundings are the ones that tend to gravitate towards food as a false means to create protection or ground our energy in order to not feel as much. Food serves as a way to shield our antennae that feels so much, that at times we can't differentiate our own feelings from the feelings of others. Some of us, if our child is angry, feel their anger as if it is our own. If our mother is sick, we feel the pain of their suffering. If our husband or wife is extremely stressed, we feel their stress. The pain that we feel in such cases isn't even our own. As such, we can easily lose touch with our own feelings because we are so sensitive to picking up the energies of all the people around us and carrying the burdens that aren't ours, but rather of our family members. Remember that we are not only digesting food, but also our emotions and those of others and the environment that we surround ourselves with. Food becomes our tool for staying grounded, though a very unhealthy tool. The extra weight that we start to carry on our body becomes a compensation for the grounding we wish to feel in our life but are having difficulty doing so naturally.

Whatever our reactions may be to life, when we overeat or eat or drink something that we know will lead us to gaining weight, we also know how we feel in our body afterwards. It may feel good to eat a piece of cake at the moment, but afterwards we may feel very sluggish with a headache. If we remember the 'after effect' of how certain foods and drinks feel, looking at their long-term impact rather than short term, it becomes easier to have the willpower to make a different choice before we succumb to the need to use food to appease our anxiety or excitement.

Anxiety not only can drive us toward the wrong choices of foods but also eating very rapidly. When we eat too quickly, we generally don't chew our food thoroughly. As such the food is not broken down fully and not digested well. This in turn weakens our digestive system and can lead to bloating, constipation and weight gain.

Gaining weight usually started at a certain time in our life. It's important to reflect on our lives and see the patterns that we carry within us from our past or even our family's past and when it started for us. What was going on in our life at that time? How is it still impacting our life today? Are we still in the same circumstances? What is causing us to overeat? What is lacking in our life? If we know that we are eating out of anxiety, what is the root of it and how can we turn the reaction of overeating into a source of power in our life? If we are using food to ground us, what can we do to feel more grounded naturally, rather than using food? Self-reflection gives us greater willpower in the long run to make changes in our habits and life. Some of the exercises I will be sharing in the chapters ahead will give you new ways of dealing with the emotions and anxiety from the practices of the indigenous people.

"Anxiety is a fire with tremendous power that is encouraging us to change. Anytime the energy is repressed by eating, we are blocking this natural flow of growth and transformation by gaining weight."

- Rita Panahi, L.Ac.

#7

Energetic Weight.
Physical Weight

Our body is multi-dimensional. Beyond being a physical material existence, our body is pure energy and expanding beyond the physical body is an energy field. This field is an extension of our physical body. Both the body and the energy field are in fact energy, but in different vibrations. The body is a denser form of energy. The energy field is a subtler form. Experiences in life also have different qualities of energy.

The indigenous healers differentiate the different qualities of energy in very simple terms as heavy and light. What falls into the category of heavy and light energies? The traumas we have experienced in our life, our negative mental chatter, our negative emotions, being in an environment of the same, pain passed down through our ancestors – such things create heavy energies that leave imprints in our energy field. On the other hand, nature's energy is light. Being a reflection of divinity, nature can help us to experience the divinity and harmony within ourselves. It has the ability to help us shift the vibration of our traumas and transform the heaviness into light and remove the energetic burdens that we carry. It's only when we experience the light quality of energy that we can differentiate how heavy our energy has been all along. It's when we are in a place of complete silence where we can hear a pin drop that we know how loud our own life has been. Living our regular life as we know it, we may not recognize the difference between heavy and light energies, but once we begin to feel the pure light energy within ourselves, we can know how heavy our energy has been until now.

Because for some of us the concept of energy or an energy field is intangible, we tend to either ignore it or remain unaware of it. Yet we have all experienced encountering someone briefly and without even speaking with them, feeling drained, angry or uneasy or similarly, meeting others that give us quite the opposite feeling of joy and peace. What is happening in these situations is that our energy fields are interacting. Our energies are interacting with people, animals, and nature at all times, with or without our awareness. Life is pure energy at different levels of vibration. Depending on the extent of the interaction, imprints are left behind in our energy field. The more difficult experiences leave heavier residues behind.

The concept of energy is very much a part of the indigenous people's everyday lives. They understand that the energy field is the blueprint for the physical body. Just as a cream that is put on the skin topically gradually gets absorbed through the pores and moves into the bloodstream, so too it is with the imprints on our energy. The traumas of our life, even if they are from 20 years ago, are left as imprints, which gradually impact the physical body, our mind, our emotions and ultimately the choices we make and our quality of life.

If we fall into a puddle of mud, we would be visibly covered in mud. If we walked around for days without taking a shower, we would most certainly feel the heaviness of the mud and continue to see the mud all over our body. It's the same when it comes to traumatic experiences as well as certain environments that we have to interact with. When something painful happens to us, it's like a bucket of mud that has been dumped onto us. Even though it's not visible to our eyes, we carry on with our lives, never acknowledging the invisible mud of our traumas and pain weighing us down and affecting every aspect of our life.

One of the main reasons that we lose weight only to start gaining it back after many weeks or months of hard work is because the energy field and the patterns left in the energy field were never addressed. For example, let's say that a person faced a lot of abuse when they first started to gain weight. They may have undergone therapy, dieted and lost weight, but after some time, again they found themselves regaining what they had lost. Some of us may never have dealt with our emotional traumas or the circumstances that initiated the weight gain originally. The pain continues to impact our life as an undercurrent that we are not fully aware of and we use food as comfort to repress the pain. Others, though we may have accepted the painful events of the past, may never have been healed energetically and purified the scars of the trauma that was left behind in our energy field. Those scars pull our body back into the same patterns again. We may lose weight without having purified and realigned our energy field to our new body and we find ourselves pulled back to our original pattern of eating and wonder what went wrong, and why we can't manage to lose weight and *keep it off.*

As much as we may try to repress or forget traumas of the past, they don't completely leave our system unless we clear them or transform them energetically. Not only is this weight resulting from the experiences of our own life, but also from the blueprints that we carry of our ancestors that may be impacting us without our awareness. The traumas that our grandparents or parents have experienced, when left unhealed, can be passed onto us as energetic patterns. We may suffer from certain emotions without understanding where the root has come from. We may follow certain habits without knowing why. These are often the results of energetic patterns passed down to us from our ancestors. These blueprints in our energy field impact us and our choices as well.

All of our interactions in our daily life, from our workplace, our home environment, and our friends and relatives, impact us, whether we are sensitive enough to feel them or not. The accumulation of the energetic imprints over our lifetime continue to build with or without our awareness. Just as dust would build on a car that was left unwashed for years, our energy field accumulates the 'dust' of many years of interactions and experiences, creating heavy energy. This heavy energy weighs us down, weakening our willpower, our digestive system, and keeping us in the pattern of being overweight. The potential for being fit, thin and vital lies dormant beneath the heavy energy; however, until we transform the energetic weight, we cannot create lasting change.

Even our own thoughts and emotions leave imprints in our energy field. Depending on their quality, they can become a weight in our energy field that weighs us down or they can uplift us. Positive emotions and thoughts, being at a higher vibration and considered light energy, support us more in losing weight. On the contrary, negative thoughts and emotions block the flow, slowing down our body's ability to digest and ultimately leading us to gaining more weight.

The indigenous people see nature as light energy and as the greatest healer and purifier of energies, if we know how to work with its energy. They understand that unless the energetic weight is purified, physical changes are short lived. A strong and pure energy field results in a strong physical body and mind, with great potentials. Whatever imprints of traumas, pain and negative thoughts are left in our energy field trickle down to weigh us down and rob us of the clarity and willpower we need for losing weight, as well as preventing us from unleashing other creative gifts we may have. Even the ideas that we carry about ourselves, if they are negative, are stored in the energy field and weigh us down.

The indigenous healers are masters of working with nature's energies. Whatever we deal with on a daily basis, we learn more about. If we spend all of our time on the computer, we begin to understand how it operates. If we spend our time with cars, we understand how they operate. In the same manner, if we spend a lot of time with nature, as the indigenous healers do, we begin to understand it on a deeper level than a person who only spends time in nature occasionally. The distractions of our modern world, such as television, music, traffic, computers and so on, make it difficult to truly listen to nature. In the same way that we learn to communicate with our pets, even though we speak a different language, the indigenous people have learned to communicate with the mountains, the sun, the trees, the rivers and the sky. For them, nature is pure energy. The same way that our energies interact with the energies of others, our energy also interacts with nature's energies, but we need to learn how to use this interaction to transform our life. When we are only dealing with the heavier energies of our own or our surroundings, we lose sight of the power and lightness that we can feel if we interact instead with more pure energies, such as that of nature. They have gained the wisdom of nature's healing power through their deep and dynamic relationship with it.

"One of the main reasons that we gain weight quickly after dieting and losing weight is because we have not faced our emotions and their weight in our life."

- Rita Panahi, L.Ac.

#8

Nature's Power to Transform

Every time I traveled to the mountains in South America, I was impressed by how the indigenous men and women healers who were in their 90's could walk up and down the mountains faster than I could, without any signs of fatigue. They were full of energy, their minds were sharp, and they would even often carry extremely large bundles wrapped in a woven blanket on their back for hours on end, going up steep inclines and back down in any type of weather. I couldn't give the credit for their vitality to their diet alone because it was extremely simple, yet their strength and stamina was greater than someone half their age. Very little grows at such high altitudes. They were not taking the newest supplement or energy drink. They were not eating large meals. Yet they were strong and full of energy.

They explained to me that their energy comes from their connection with the earth and all of nature. Transforming their heavy energies with nature's power is what allows their mind to be clear, and their body to be strong and vital. They believe that most people have lost touch with nature as a result of their lifestyle and are dependant on all sorts of special foods, supplements and vitamins for energy, yet they are still tired and run down. One of the main factors for being so run down is the accumulation of heavy energies in their energy field. The different elements of nature have different qualities and powers to help ground us, cleanse our energy field, break up the blockages, heal our traumas, balance our system, clear our mind and more. It's the interrelationship with nature that people have forgotten, taking nature for granted in many ways, and not working together with nature for their own survival and for their own healing that has led to many of the problems they face in their lives. Nature is the most abundant healer, but people walk on the earth without realizing its innate power. They see the sun, but only on their holidays to get a tan. They see a tree, but use it to climb upon or cut it down. They see a mountain and see it as a challenge to reach its peak. They see the moon and think of it as a sign for nighttime having arrived. They fail to recognize nature as the ultimate teacher and healer. Nature is the secret to healing one's past, transforming oneself, finding peace within and reaching one's true nature. By connecting to specific energies of nature, the indigenous healers are able to transform their energy field by clearing the imbalances and heaviness.

Imbalances in the energy field create imbalances in our physical body. The energy field has a direct impact on the body and is like a filter that sends clear or distorted messages to the physical body. If the energy field is heavy, it weighs down the body. We are rarely taught how to clear these traumas from our life on ALL levels so that we can truly heal and have our full vitality in life. Through their practices with nature, the indigenous healers transform their heavy energy to light. They shift the vibration of their energy by cleansing the energy body.

Living a fast-paced life, we have lost our connection with nature. Even those of us who may appreciate nature by spending more time outdoors backpacking and trekking, oftentimes see it more as a test of our endurance to dominate the forces of nature rather than be in harmony with them. And those that have come to love nature and care for the environment have not learned how to connect with the energy of nature specifically for their own healing.

No human can stop the forces of an earthquake, a hurricane, an avalanche, a flash flood. No human can stop the sun from shining or the rain from falling. Nature follows its law of existence. It can continue to exist and renew in other forms continuously with or without humans. However, without nature, we as humans could not exist. Without the sun, we would freeze and crops would not be able to grow. Without trees, we would not be able to breathe. Without water, no crops would grow and we would not be able to survive for long. The indigenous people understand their dependence on nature and pay great respect and reverence to it and as such understand its power, not only for survival but also for healing. Living in such remote areas with little distractions, they listen to the silence within nature and have developed a deeper relationship with it. In a city, without the sun shining, we can go inside our house and turn on the heat to stay warm. In the remote mountains, without the sun shining, we would still feel the cold if we did not have access to heat in the simple homes, as the indigenous people live in. In the city, if we are looking for food, we go to the market and find what we need, even if it is grown in countries far away from where we live. In the mountains, if the weather conditions aren't right, we may not be able to grow or harvest sufficient food for our survival. First we must see the importance of nature, in order to develop a deep reverence for it, then we must connect to its energy to develop a deep relationship with it.

How do we go about connecting with nature and healing ourselves with nature? We are all connected - humans, animals, and all of nature. The same way that we connect with another human by meeting them, thinking about them or calling them, it all starts with the intention to do so. Nature understands us and communicates with us energetically when we connect with our intention. The same way that people who have pets communicate with their pets though the pets don't speak the human language, so too can we communicate with the river, the trees, the mountain, the sun. A tree will hear us. The sun will hear us. The earth will understand us. The wind will understand us. The ocean will hear us. All of nature hears and understands our heart and mind and replies to us. We simply need to be silent to hear the language it speaks, the language of the heart. What is important in healing is that we connect with nature in a state of humility and surrender of the heart.

The sun that gives light to our life and helps plants to grow can also help our energy field to be filled with strength and purified of the unhealthy blueprints. The earth that transforms the fallen leaves of a tree into soil has the ability to draw the heavy energy of our traumas and suffering into its core and transform our pain. By lightening our energetic weight, it supports us in losing the physical weight that we carry and opening us up to our creativity for inspiration to fill our life.

Nature is a reflection of divinity. These practices I will be sharing in the following chapters are to help you to connect with the power of nature, the spirit of nature that is all around you. They are best done outdoors in nature, but when this is not possible, they can also be done anywhere through visualization. Remember that nature is alive and pure love and beingness. It has tremendous healing powers. The spirit of nature knows your heart. The more you connect through your heart, the more you will receive back. Love, a word that is extremely overused and misunderstood, is a magical energy and nature is pure love. With nature there is no ego, nor a mind that discriminates. It is only giving of itself at all times. Every step that we take towards nature with love, it gives back to us energetically 10 times more. This is the key to transforming our energy while in the process of working towards losing weight.

As you read through the different exercises, see which element calls you first. Are your drawn to the tree for balancing? Are you drawn to the sky for clarity? Are you more drawn to the earth for grounding? Are you drawn to water for clearing and vitalizing your energy? All are powerful and all can be done at different times, but start with the one that you feel most drawn to, either because you feel the greatest affinity with that element of nature or because of the healing power that it holds.

Nature is without mind and connects us to our deepest inner self, the divinity within our self. When we learn how to work with the energies of nature, we can learn to purify our energy and transform the vibration so that when it comes to losing weight, we can have more lasting results. As you begin your new relationship with nature, approach it with gratitude and thankfulness. Any time that you feel you are off balance or heavy energetically, take 5 minutes before you go to bed or when you wake up, and connect to the spirit of the desired element of nature. It is rare that we overeat when we are feeling in harmony within ourselves and our environment. Overeating in itself is a sign of not being in harmony with ourselves or our environment. The key is to realign our energy with that of nature in order to realign ourselves and find peace and harmony within ourselves.

"It is rare that we over eat when we are feeling in harmony within ourselves and our environment. Over eating in itself is a sign of not being in harmony with ourselves or our environment. The key is to realign our energy with that of nature in order to realign ourselves and find peace and harmony within ourselves."

- Rita Panahi, L.Ac.

#9

Transforming Energies Through Shamanic Practices

Beyond being critical for our survival, nature is a mystery that can only be tapped into through a deep connection with its energy or spirit. And a true, sincere connection can only happen when it comes from the heart, with humility and love. Every part of nature has a life-force, a spirit, that is alive and that hears and understands the silent language of our soul. It is best to develop this relationship with the innocence of a child. Open your heart and speak with it as you would with your dearest friend. If at any point emotions surface that make you feel uneasy, ask the element of nature you are working with to help you heal and cleanse those emotions. If you still feel overwhelmed, then simply stop for the time being, and try again at a later time. You may also want to try to work with a different element instead.

The practices I will be sharing are done outdoors in nature by the indigenous healers, however feel free to do them either outdoors or at home using your intention. No matter where you are, they simply require your intention to connect. At first they may appear very simple, yet they are extremely profound. The more frequently you do them, the more you will experience their effect. They can be done for just 5 minutes or longer if you have the time. Do not strain yourself while doing the practices. Adjust your position or location so that you are completely comfortable. To begin with you may be putting aside time specifically to do the practices, but you may find that you can do them no matter where you are or at any time, once you feel more comfortable. You can be walking outdoors and use your intention to connect to the sun. You could be at your desk at work and use your intention to connect with the spirit of the sky. You could be waiting for someone to arrive at a coffee shop and connect to the spirit of the sky. You can feel the love and power of nature within you at all times to help realign you and give you the clarity, strength, grounding, or vision that you need. Nature is your best friend if you allow it to be.

There are practices with numerous energies of nature, the earth, the sun, the waterfall, the river, the mountain, the tree, and the sky. Choose the one that you need at any given point. You may work with one element for some time or try various ones to experience the difference. As you spend more and more time with nature, it will reveal more of its magic and wisdom to you. Know that nature is the expression of divinity and purity and that it's a reflection of your innate nature. When you are in alignment with nature, you are in alignment with your deepest self. When you are in balance, your choices are healthy, your willpower is strong, and your mind is clear. When your foundation is in alignment, weight loss becomes effortless.

Earth

When the leaves fall from the trees, they start to decompose and the earth transforms them into the soil. The seeds that are planted in the soil of the earth are brought to life within the womb of the earth as they sprout and begin to reach up towards the sky. The earth is like a womb that gives life. The earth transforms energies. It can take the heavy energy from your pain into its womb, transform it and lighten your energy and heart. It draws your energy into its core to ground you the same way that it holds the roots of the trees and keeps them stable as they reach for the sky.

This is a great practice to clear accumulations of heavy energies. It is also very beneficial to help to ground your energy when you feel anxious or stressed. It can be done daily and its best done in daylight. In the dark, other energies are present and can interfere with the cleansing process.

Exercise ~

Lie face down on the earth. Expose your belly button and lower abdomen so that it touches the grass or the soil you are laying on. If you are concerned about the earth getting on your clothing, place down two towels, one for your upper body and one for the lower so that your belly button remains exposed to the earth, touching it. Feel the earth against your face and body. Feel its heartbeat. Feel it supporting you. Take a few deep breaths as you let your body relax. See the area of your belly button opening to the earth and all of the heavy energy of your pain, traumas, sadness, worries, and anger falling into the earth. If anyone has hurt you, see it being drawn down through the opening of your belly button into the earth. Feel the earth pulling all of the heavy energy from your entire body, from your head and your toes going towards the belly button and down into the earth. Feel your body and your energy becoming lighter as the weight you have been carrying falls away. Scan your body, your shoulders, neck, head, chest, arms, genitals, thighs, feet, and hands. See if there are any more residues of heavy energy or blockages that need to be cleared and allow them all to be pulled down into the earth through the opening of your belly button. Feel the earth as a mother that takes away all your pain, leaving you filled with love. Take a few deep breaths and once you feel complete, brush the palm of your hand over the opening of your belly button as if to close the opening and cut any remaining debris left hanging. Gently kiss the earth and come to a sitting position on your knees. Thank the earth as you bow down and touch your forehead to the earth. Let the earth clear your mind of all negative thoughts and worry. Pray that the earth clears your mind and gives you strength and compassion for yourself as well as for others.

Sun

The sun is a powerful force of light, which brings about growth, vitality, clarity and lightness. It clears the darkness and suffering within our life, shifting our vibration to a higher level. The sun gives strength and energy to move forward with our visions and dreams. Just as it gives the energy for seeds to sprout and grow, it gives energy for the seeds of our creativity to blossom and removes the obstructions that stand in their way. The indigenous healers say that we are all 'children of the sun', meaning that the sun is a true reflection of who we are. By connecting to the sun, we find our way back to our true power.

This practice can be done while sitting, standing or laying down on your back. If the sun shines through your bedroom window, you can lie in your bed and allow the rays to shine on you as you do the practice. If it is visible from your balcony, you can sit there. You can stand in your garden or in the park and do this practice. It can be done wherever you can see the sun and you feel peaceful. When it's not possible to actually see the sun, do the practice visualizing the sun.

Know that even if you are walking outside running your errands, you can connect to the sun at any time and bring its light within you. You only need a few seconds of your intention to feel your connection. If you are feeling down, if you are feeling off balance, ask the sun to help you with its light and clear your energy with its rays.

Exercise ~

See the sun shining above you. Close your eyes and be receptive. Take a few breaths in and out. Feel the warmth of the sun as its rays touch your body. Like a brush stroke, let the rays begin clearing your energy field surrounding your body from your head all the way to your toes. Feel your body becoming lighter as the golden rays clear and replace the heaviness. Take a deep breath and allow the rays to gradually penetrate through your skin entering into your body, and in the same way, brushing away all of the darkness, the heaviness and pain, and leaving behind a golden luminous light. Allow the rays to touch every part of your body, every cell, clearing the darkness from the outside and inside. Let the rays linger a little longer in the areas that feel blocked and allow them to slowly break up the darkness, stagnation and pain of the past. See yourself filled with golden light and the light expanding from the inside of your body back out filling your body and your energy field. You are filled with light within and surrounded by light. Feel the strength of the sun within you, filling you with its energy and vitality and moving up your spine from the sacrum up to the neck and out from the top of the head, clearing away any left-over darkness from your entire spine.

Feel the peace within you and now see the sun's light moving from your head back down through your body to your feet and into the earth. Take a few deep breaths in and out, feeling strong and grounded being filled with the sun's light. Remain with this experience for a little while and when you feel complete, bow down to the sun and thank it for its tremendous gift of light and its power.

Water

Water is a powerful and unique part of nature with its ability to transform from liquid to vapor to liquid to ice. It can be gentle and soft or rough and forceful. Water touches the earth and the sky by changing form. With its ability to change form, it carries the energies of both heaven and earth. The waters in the oceans evaporate into the sky, becoming the clouds. The clouds move through the sky and rain back down into fields and rivers. The water that was in the rivers of one country can be the same water that evaporates and becomes the clouds raining in the rivers of another country far away. Water cleanses our body when we drink. Its molecules help our body's metabolism. Our body consists of approximately 70% water. Water gives us life as it flows through our body through our bloodstream, in the same way that it nourishes the crops, trees and plants to grow as it flows in the rivers of the earth. The flow of water can purify and cleanse us as it carries us in its fluid arms. Water not only helps to clean our physical body, but can also purify our energy. It can carry us to the mystery of who we are.

This practice can be done with an actual waterfall or river if you are close to one or through visualization.

Waterfall

Exercise ~

Imagine yourself standing in front of a gentle waterfall. It's a beautiful warm day. As you stand facing the waterfall, allow yourself to become receptive. Hear its sound and feel the water gently spraying against your body. Slowly begin walking towards the waterfall through the very shallow pond in front of you. Feel the firm earth beneath your feet. Have your palms open facing the waterfall and feel the spray of water even more as you walk closer. The water is warm and you stand under the waterfall. The force of the water is soft as it comes over your body from your head down to your toes, like a gentle invigorating shower.

Feeling the water washing over your body, ask the waterfall to cleanse you of your pain and suffering, of all of your heavy energy that you have been carrying for all of these years. Feel the waterfall purifying your energy field. Feel it falling on your chest over your heart center and clearing away the sadness, the grief, and the hurt that you have been carrying. Feel your body becoming lighter as it washes away your pain and fills your body with vitality. You feel more energized, lighter and more joyful. You are vibrating with life.

When you feel complete, walk out from under the waterfall. Look back and send your prayers of thanks for its healing life force. Whenever you feel heavy and tired, connect with the spirit of the waterfall and allow it to help clear the heaviness and fill you with energy and vitality.

River

Exercise ~

See yourself sitting next to a gentle river. The water is crystal clear and you can see the rocks at the bottom of the river. The water is flowing smoothly and you can hear its soothing sound. It's a warm day and the sun is shining above you. You are surrounded by the beauty and silence of nature as you listen to the water flowing in the river. You feel the sound and the flow in your heart as you sit beside the river and it draws you to step inside the water.

You walk into the river that comes up to your hips and feel the water flowing gently against your legs as you begin praying to the spirit of the river. Ask the river to cleanse you of all the heaviness in your life, to remove all of the pain of your past and your present. Anything anyone has done to you, ask the river to wash it away. Any hurt that you carry towards others or yourself - jealousy, hate, anger, sadness - whatever you are carrying deep within you, ask the river to wash it away. Imagine all of the people or situations that are causing you discomfort and pain, all of the misunderstandings and discord, ask for it all to be washed away. Once you have completed your prayers to the spirit of the river, enter into the flowing water with your entire body. See a large rock in front of you under the water where your feet are, and use that as your anchor as you lie in the river floating and the crystal clear, pure water washing over your body. Your feet against the rock hold you in place. As you float in the river the water answers your prayers by washing away everything that has weighed your down. It continues to flow over you until you feel light and energized.

When you feel ready, stand up once again and thank the river from your heart in gratitude. Slowly walk back out onto the bank of the river feeling refreshed, renewed, joyful, light, and vital.

Mountain

Mountains carry the energy of solid strength and stability. The indigenous healers say that the peaks of the mountains connect to the stars. They say that the mountains have the wisdom of years stored within them both of the stars and the earth. With all of the changes that take place on the earth, the mountains stand solid. The power of the mountain brings grounding, strength and a deep inner wisdom into our energy. When you feel weak or too sensitive to your surroundings and you need strength and protection, connect with the mountain from your heart and allow its spirit to support you.

Exercise ~

Sit comfortably or lie down in a relaxed position. Imagine that you are on a mountain. It can be at the bottom of the mountain, along its path or at the top. See the vast view in front of you. Take a few deep breaths in and out and experience the silence and peace around you. The sky is clear above you. The weather is pleasantly warm. Feel the gentle wind against your skin as you sit on the mountain. Speak with the mountain and allow your heart to connect to its energy.

See a tube entering into the mountain from your sacrum (the bottom of your spine) and allow the energy of the mountain to move up through your spine. Feel your body becoming as strong as the mountain with deep inner silence and strength. Allow your mind to be empty. Sit with the mountains power for as long as you need to. Anywhere in your body that you may have felt weak, let the mountain fill it with its power. When you are complete, bow down to the mountain. Thank it for sharing its strength so generously with you.

Tree

Trees are a bridge between heaven and earth. Their deep roots help to ground us, while their branches help us to reach beyond our narrow vision and expand to new horizons. The trunk helps us to learn to be balanced within our own energy. Many times when we gain weight, it is because we are not grounded enough to have the strength to say no and make the right choices. We can feel like a feather that is blown left and right without control. Other people, our own emotions, and external circumstances can all throw us off balance. The roots of the tree are very powerful to teach us how to keep our roots strong in the earth in all circumstances and allow the heaviness in our life to be pulled into the earth and cleared from our energy field so that we don't carry the burden. The power of the tree is to bring balance, grounding and vision.

Exercise ~

Stand next to a tree. It can be any kind of tree that you love the most. Touch its trunk with love and gentleness as if you are meeting an old dear friend. Know the spirit of the tree feels your presence and feels your touch. Stand straight with your spine and head against the tree and feel the strength of the tree behind you, standing firmly with its roots in the ground. Let your spine merge with the trunk of the tree and feel the tree clearing your spine of the histories of your pain. Feel your spine vibrating with the energy of the tree, from the sacrum all the way up to your neck and head. The tree is drawing in all of the heaviness of your pain that has been stored in your spine and weighing you down your entire life, into its trunk and down into its roots. Take a few deep breaths and continue to feel the tree healing you, clearing away your heavy energies.

Once you feel that your spine has been cleared, turn and face the tree putting your arms around the trunk and press your body against it, lovingly holding the tree in your embrace. Let your forehead lean against the tree and allow your body to merge with the tree. Feel it clearing the heavy energies from the front of your body, pulling all of the darkness into its trunk and sending it through its roots to the earth. Feel your mind clearing and your vision expanding. See a tube going from between your legs deep into the earth and at the same time a tube going from the top of your head up towards the sky while you are still holding your arms around the tree. Feel yourself as a vessel between heaven and earth with your feet deeply rooted in the earth. Above your head, the cord is expanding to the sky, bringing in the inspiration for new visions. Your heart opens to love and is filled with peace from the tree's presence. Just as the tree gives its love freely, you become an antenna receiving and giving love from your heart. You are the bridge between heaven and earth and your heart is the source of giving and receiving love with the world around you. Feel yourself in harmony with nature, balanced, strong and clear. Take a few deep breaths in and out and when you feel complete, slowly step away from the tree as you touch it with love, thanking its spirit for helping you to heal.

Sky

The sky is infinite, expanding beyond what we see and can even imagine. It is an endless, vast space. Sometimes when we have worries or pain, our vision can become very narrow and limited, as does our energy field. The flow within our body and mind becomes restricted due to our tensions, pain and thoughts, which block the harmonious flow in our body and life. The sky is pure space. It is within space that there can be flow. It is within expansion that there can be the possibility of new opportunities and new perceptions. To see ourselves different than we are, we need to allow more space for new energies to flow through our life. The sky allows for this expansion and flow.

Exercise ~

Sit comfortably or lie down. Close your eyes and begin to see the beautiful vast blue sky above you. Take a few deep breaths in and out and begin to see the sky filling your entire body. You become the sky and the sky expands from your body, where you and the sky are merged together. Feel the vastness, the peace and silence. Breathe deeply and as you breathe in and out, see the sky breathing in and out within you. You are the sky. The sky is within you and expanding out from you. When experiencing the expansion, memories of pains and uncomfortable feelings may surface. The feelings may keep our energy tight, but breathe into those feelings and allow the sky to fill the areas of tightness slowly. If the feeling is overwhelming to deal with, then just allow it to be for the time being and put your attention on the rest of your body being filled with the vast sky. Allow the expansion to the point that feels comfortable to you. Each time as you heal more and release the energy blocks, you will be able to allow the sky to expand from your body and further out into the infinite space.

Feel the peace and lightness in this space and ask the spirit of the sky to help you with the direction and visions of your life. Ask the sky to show you your potential, whether it's your work, your relationship, or your body. Let your mind expand and see the new you that the sky is showing you. See your body. See yourself healthy. See yourself fit and vital. See your body weight exactly how you wish it to be. Look at your face and see the joy on your face. Feel how good it feels to be light. Feel the creativity that you have been leaving dormant within you now slowly emerging out from within you. Wonderful ideas and visions for your future surface from the depth of who you are. Allow the excitement and joy of your new life, the new you, to start to flow, guiding you to the next steps that you need to take, to make them all a reality in your life. Take a deep breath in and out. Fill your lungs, fill your body with the breath of the sky, the expansion of the sky. When you feel complete, slowly open your eyes. Looking out at the sky, bow down in gratitude and thank the spirit of the sky. Know that the sky is guiding you towards your vision.

"Unless the energetic weight is purified, physical changes are often temporary."

- Rita Panahi, L.Ac.

#10

The Power Behind Weight: Unleash Your Creativity

Until recently, we may have focused mainly on our body, trying different diets and exercising in order to lose weight. We have probably faced disappointment and frustration at some point, either because it was difficult to lose weight or because the results were short lived. We kept changing our exercise routine and our diet, believing they hold the key to finally losing weight permanently. We may never have thought of losing weight as it relates to the emotions or our energy or even our ancestral energy. As such we may never have addressed these when we were trying to lose weight, and found ourselves drawn back once again by the patterns imprinted in our energy field. As a result, we have felt hopeless in achieving our goal and being able to maintain it. Losing weight is seen by most of us as a demon to overcome. Yet, it has rarely been viewed as a tremendous gift of latent potential hidden within us.

What is weight in truth? It's true that eating the wrong foods, eating too much food and lack of exercise can all lead to us gaining weight. It is true that our emotions and stress can throw us off balance, causing us to overeat and gain weight. It's true that the traumas and pains of our past, our daily interactions, our negative thoughts all leave imprints in our energy field that weigh us down, weakening our digestive system and our willpower, leading us to overeat and gain weight.

Yet no matter what has led us to gaining weight, weight is a form of stored energy. Hidden within that stored energy is tremendous power and creativity just waiting to be released. When we try to lose weight, we are trying to get rid of something that can come back like a boomerang that we have thrown away. However, when we transform our weight, we allow for another power to be awakened from the weight.

Food, rather than being seen as medicine, is often used as a means to repress our feelings, stress, anxiety, sadness, or anger. But in truth, these feelings cannot remain repressed. Doing so only contains them within our body like a volcano ready to erupt at the most unexpected moments, sometimes at others and other times even against ourselves. All emotions are a form of energy and when we repress them, they do not go away but linger in our energy field, creating blocks for the flow within our life. As long as they remain as a block, weighing us down, they cause many disturbances and imbalances in many aspects of our life and mind, including our weight. The blocks gradually slow down our digestion and lead to weight gain and other complications but when released, they are a tremendous force that can be directed towards creativity, growth and change in our life. We need to see the weight that we have gained as a hidden treasure and a source for hidden potential just waiting to be opened.

Life is pure energy. Our body, our food, our emotions, our thoughts, and our experiences are all different forms of energy. To lose weight, to transform our life, we need to transform the heavy energies that weigh us down in order for the physical changes to last. Sometimes, if we lose too much weight too quickly, it can lead to too much energy being released too quickly. If we are not ready to deal with them, we can feel overwhelmed and frightened, and regress back to our pattern of overeating to repress the energy. That is the reason why it's beneficial to have a plan for directing the energy as we are losing weight to allow the flow towards our creativity.

We may have many visions and hopes, but out of fear or lack of self-confidence we ignore them, believing that we can never achieve them or that we can never be the person that we wish to become. We need to ask ourselves, what is it that we want to create in our life? What fears do we have that prevent us from reaching our goal? Those are the fears that we repress with junk food, alcohol, and overeating.

The hidden power within weight is an amazing creative force. As we begin to lose weight, we allow the energy to flow and flourish. It's important to go deep within ourselves and reflect on our life, from the time that we were a child until today, and see what some of the things have been that made us happy but we never did them out of fear or other reasons. Did we enjoy painting? Did we love to travel the world? Did we always long to have our own business? Did we always want to create with our hands? Did we want to invent something? Did we enjoy dancing? Did we want to write? Look for things that you had wanted to do as a means of expressing your deeper longings that you never pursued. These longings don't have to be ways of making a living, though they certainly could be, but passions that have been left unexplored. It's about remembering what gave us joy yet we left it behind. It is those things that have been buried deep within us that are preventing our creative force from coming to life. It's about letting the magic that has been hidden inside of us, the longing that has been in our soul, to start to show its face and begin to move and express itself in positive ways in our life, rather than being pushed under the rug as we gain weight. Our pain, anger, sadness, fear, worry - all can be transformed to a lighter energy that allows us to turn our life around. It's about energy continuing to move and being directed to move in the direction of our creativity.

There are many seeds of inspiration and passion hidden within us. However, throughout our life, people may have told us that we are not good enough. People may have done something to make us feel that we are incapable. People may have hurt us, making us lose hope. No matter what has happened, the seeds of our creativity remain dormant within us. Unless we give them the space and opportunity to grow, we will have to fight a constant battle of repressing them, at the expense of our body, our weight, and our health. Movement is life. By allowing for movement in our metabolism, in our emotions, in our energy, we are invoking our life force to be allowed to move freely and we need to have a plan to direct it towards our vision, our dreams, and our creativity. Have a dream and vision in mind *before* starting to lose weight.

As contrary as it may sound, feeling joy is sometimes the greatest fear that we have. Out of guilt, out of habit, out of fear, we do not allow joy to be present in our life. We need to first give ourselves permission to be joyful. We need to feel comfortable with joy. Joy is a high vibration. It helps to improve our metabolism. It helps us to create new dreams. It gives us the energy we need to follow our dreams. Joy is not something that we feel only when we have something or someone, but rather a feeling deep within ourselves irrespective of circumstances. Joy and peace go hand in hand. They are a state of being that we can cultivate within. All of the practices that we talked about, from the indigenous healer's perspective, are to help remove the obstacles that prevent us from experiencing this deep joy. Nature's energies are what allow for the blockages to be removed, our energy to be clear and in alignment and for there to be flow towards our potential. The presence of the indigenous people was filled with joy, peace and vitality, even though their life circumstances were much more difficult and harsh than one could ever imagine. Nature was the key to their state of being and vitality.

When putting so much emphasis on losing weight we often forget our real focus: to be healthy, to live our potential, to find peace. Losing weight does not give us peace. Peace will help us to lose weight. Losing weight will not bring happiness. Happiness will help us make healthy choices so that we lose weight. Our goal should not only be to lose weight, but rather to have a goal to fulfill our dreams and feel joy and peace within. Weight loss will become the fuel that will push us towards our dreams and creativity as it releases the creative life force that is stored within the cells of the body. If left untouched, the weight slows us down and takes away our strength and hope. But as we begin to lose weight, as the creativity gets unleashed, our connection with our higher self increases. Our higher self is our source of inspiration, joy, and peace and the relationship with nature is the bridge. Nature is a reflection of love and it's in this state of love that we can find peace and joy within.

Love is what truly heals our body, mind and spirit. To diet without loving ourselves will only lead to temporary weight loss. Gaining weight is a sign of imbalance of the relationship with ourselves and with nature. If we buy a ring that we absolutely love, we will do everything in our power to take care not to lose it. If we buy a car that we love, we will wash it, wax it, clean it, drive it with care and maintain it in perfect condition. How we live, what we put in our body, and who we spend time with are all reflections of the love we feel toward ourselves. We will give our body the best only if we feel how important it is. We will fill our body with junk only if we don't care enough about ourselves and our well-being. Loving ourselves is not about how others treat us, but about how we take care of ourselves. To ignore the signs our body is giving us is to ignore ourselves. If we are having pain, whether emotional or physical, it is our body saying it needs attention and care. If we are gaining weight, it is our body saying it is overwhelmed.

Weight no longer has to be an enemy that we battle with, but rather a treasure chest of passions and creativity. To unleash the creativity, we need to simply clear the path by clearing our emotions and energy field along with our physical body. Only then will weight loss be a complete process of transformation, not only for our body, but for our spirit and life as well. Our greatest healer and teacher on the journey is nature's powerful energy.

Let's begin the journey together beginning a new relationship with nature to create our new life, living in harmony and peace with ourselves and nature, in order to lose weight and unleash the seeds of our dreams into reality.

"We need to learn how to connect with nature's healing power to transform our weight and our life."

- Rita Panahi, L.Ac.

My Journey

Similar to most people who have struggled with their weight, for the first half of my life, I constantly gained and lost weight only to gain again. At the time, I never thought about food in terms of calories or whether what I was eating was healthy. I ate only what I enjoyed eating without too much thought. I loved sweets, ice cream, chocolate, milkshakes and donuts, and ate them without hesitation. I didn't understand food as nourishment for my body, because I didn't know that that's what food was actually for. If I enjoyed the taste, I would eat it. In my late teens, I began exercising and that countered the excessive calories I was taking in through sweets, but when I would stop for a period of time, I would once again gain weight. Exercise was a form of distraction from my addiction to sweets and from dealing with my emotions. I realized I had problems with weight, but I didn't realize I had a problem with food, my emotions, my mind or that they played any role in my weight fluctuation. I didn't understand what being healthy meant and subsequently didn't make healthy choices with food. My concern was mainly with my weight rather than my health. Any time that I felt stressed, sad or experienced discomforts in my life, I turned to food. If it was labeled as food and if I liked it, I assumed it was good to eat. I wasn't happy with my body weight but I felt helpless, having neither enough knowledge nor willpower to make different and better choices.

The direction of my life was about to change after waking up from a dream where I found myself in the mountains in a land that I couldn't recognize. It wasn't so much the mountains alone that woke me from my sleep, but the energy that I felt in my body being there. I felt vibrant, light, happy and filled with strength. Since I always loved traveling and had already traveled quite a bit, I wondered if the place I had seen in my dream actually existed. I began doing some research and was surprised to find images of the Andes Mountains in South America and the people being very similar to those I had seen in my dream. The following year I was off on a trip to South America. At the time, the purpose of the journey was more out of curiosity than anything else, yet in hindsight, it led to experiences and a transformation in my life that I had never expected nor imagined.

I embarked on my trip alone, meeting up with a local guide upon arrival who took me to the mountains. We began the journey by car, driving all day to a small village in the mountains. The following day at 4 a.m., we drove yet another 2 hours to an even smaller village beyond which there was no longer any access by car. From there we continued on foot, walking through rugged terrain, accompanied by snow, hail, rain, strong winds, fog and freezing cold weather along the mountain passes. For a person who was not too fond of nature at the time, it was quite an experience, filled with fear, wonder, and anxiety. By 7pm, just before sundown, we reached our destination - two stone huts in the middle of the vast mountain range and nothing else in sight. Two families of indigenous people lived there at 16,000 ft altitude.

The ten days that I spent there completely changed my view on life and nature. The life that the indigenous people were living was incredibly simple. Their relationship with nature was profound. Their stamina to walk up and down the mountains for long hours with no fatigue was admirable. Their perception of life and relationship with nature was very different than anything I had ever experienced. They loved nature the way a mother loves her child, with the same care and respect. And they honored nature the way a student honors their most respected teacher, with reverence and humility.

Nature's power was very palpable in the silence and vastness of the mountains. Since I was very young, I had always been afraid of being in nature. Being alone in the dark under the stars at night was frightening. Swimming in the ocean where I couldn't see the bottom was terrifying. I was afraid to be alone in the mountains. I was very much a city girl with very little relationship with nature. Nature's power and mystery intimidated me. I had the need to be in control and nature was where I felt I could not be in control. But life can place experiences on our path, which can change us in ways we never expected. This experience with the indigenous healers was one of those life-altering experiences that not only changed my relationship with nature and the course of my life, but also changed my weight once and for all.

Upon returning to my regular life, I found myself losing weight easily and naturally without any struggles. I felt as if a huge energetic weight had been lifted from my shoulders and more than 20 years later, the weight that I lost has still been maintained with very little effort. I attribute this to the teachings that were shared with me in the mountains, some of which I have shared with you.

Throughout the years, I returned back to South America on numerous occasions and continued to learn from the indigenous healers. In addition, I pursued a Masters in Chinese Medicine where I enhanced my knowledge about food as medicine, healing naturally and the importance of health.

The constant fluctuations in my weight had finally come to a halt once I had developed a new relationship with nature and learned how to work with its energy. The practices not only cleared the imbalances in my energy but put me in alignment to live a healthy life that supported losing weight. My life had shifted from being unaware of the power of food and the importance of health, having very little willpower to make the necessary changes to lose weight, living a constant struggle between gaining and losing weight, and being fearful of and disconnected from nature, to a complete change in perception and understanding. The relationship with nature and the understanding of the numerous dimensions to weight loss transformed my body and well being to develop an innate signal to be in balance and make healthy choices.

Subsequently, there is not a day that goes by where I am not aware of nature. It doesn't matter if I am in the suburbs or in a busy city, there is always the sky above, the sun, some trees and the earth, no matter where I travel to. I am aware that my life depends on nature and every morning when I wake up and every evening before going to bed, I bow down to it. I sense a constant exchange of energy and love between myself and nature and it's through this relationship that the excess weight was finally lost. I share my journey with you to inspire you to learn to find balance in your life and body through developing a relationship with nature so that you can lose weight and be healthy.

Stay Connected

www.facebook.com/RitaPanahiAuthor

www.facebook.com/groups/RitaPanahiAuthor

RitaPanahiAuthor

@RitaAuthor

www.ritapanahi.com

Wishing you happiness and peace as you embark on your journey to not only lose weight, but to transform your life. There is nothing more precious than your health, which includes your body, your mind, your emotions and your energy. May you feel the love from nature all around you supporting you to love yourself and take good care of yourself. And may your new relationship with nature open your heart and the pathway to success to *Lose Weight and Unleash Your Creativity* towards the life that you always dreamed of.

With love,
Rita Panahi, L.Ac.

About the Author

Rita Panahi, **L.Ac., Dipl.O.M.,** holds a Masters in Chinese Medicine with 3000+ hours of pre and post-Masters training. Over the past decade she has trained under renowned masters in the ancient teachings of Chinese Medicine rarely found in traditional training programs. She is licensed by the California Acupuncture Board, New York Board and the National Commission of Acupuncture and Oriental Medicine. In addition, for the past two decades, she has trained with indigenous healers in various countries of South America.

She has compiled her knowledge and strategies found within *Lose Weight Unleash Your Creativity* based on her vast experience and travels over the years.

Also available by **Rita Panahi, L.Ac.**

"How to Change Your Karma Now"

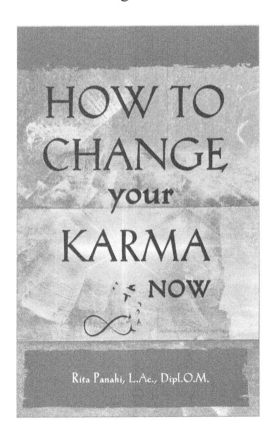

Also available by **Rita Panahi, L.Ac.**

"Own Your Health Change Your Destiny"

Made in United States
North Haven, CT
24 March 2023

34505782R00104